BREAS...

Of Judgement:
Choshen

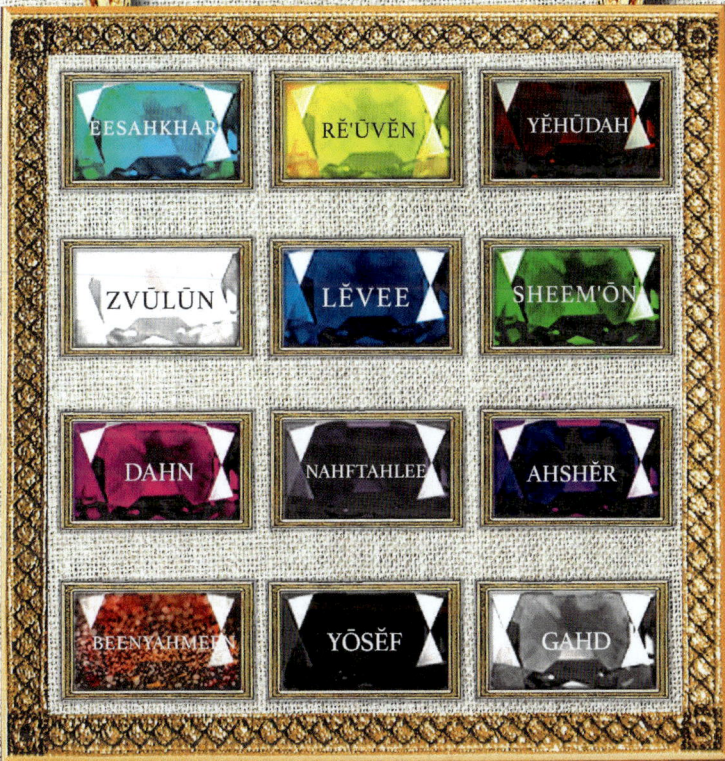

'EESAHKHAR

RĔ'ÜVĔN

YĔHŪDAH

ZVŪLŪN

LĔVEE

SHEEM'ŌN

DAHN

NAHFTAHLEE

AHSHĔR

BEENYAHMEEN

YŌSĔF

GAHD

Pamela S. Cabell

Published by Purpose Publishing
1503 Main Street #168 ❧ Grandview, Missouri
www.purposepublishing.com

ISBN: 978-09903010-0-4

Cover design by: Thaddeus Jordan
Editing by: Frank Kresen

Printed in the United States of America

This book is available at quantity discounts for bulk
purchases, inquiries may be addressed to:
www.55nuggetsofgold.com

-

*Scripture used in this book are noted
from the KJV of the Bible*

DEDICATION

To my Heavenly Father, my Savior and Elder Brother Jesus, and precious Holy Spirit — comforter and friend. In you I live, in you I move, and in you I have my existence. Life is good because of you.

To my family — both natural and spiritual. Because of your constant encouragement, prayers, love (including needed correction), and even financial support, this dream has become a reality.

Specifically some that I will name: Sandra A. Saddler (mom), Henry W. Patrick (dad), Kevin T. Cabell (father of our children), Sione N. Cabell (firstborn and daughter), Solomon H. Cabell (eldest son), and Symeon T. Cabell (youngest son). — and a host of other family members too many to name. It is because of you that I've found purpose and identity. I may not always share enough, but I value our relationships more than you know.

There are a few key people with whom I've shared a lifetime of experiences, good and bad times, multiple prayers, tears, and much laughter: Lynda A. Hall (deceased), Edith Vanderhorst Pulley, Cynthia Coley Nsiegbe, and Evangelist Louise E. Cheatham.

Lastly, this book was written for both Jews and Gentiles; however, it is as a testament to the nation of Israel — the chosen people as to the sovereignty of our God and His Christ. I am a "mother" and intercessor of Israel! May our Lord place it in your hands and may His anointing open your eyes as you read. To God be the glory.

Jesus, The Good Shepherd

CONTENTS

FOREWORD

Pamela Cabell, from the first time I met her had a hunger and a thirst for GOD. Through all the trials she encountered she never waivered in her faith or her love for God. Even as a new believer, she was faithful and had a desire to know more about God and His Word. She had a hunger for souls and a heart for sharing God with others. I am not surprised that God chosen her to write this book, the "Breastplate of Judgment". She is committed to the vision God has given her concerning his people. In her darkest valley she held on to her faith. She was committed to the mission and put her trust in the Lord. Pam validates how vital it is to keep your Breastplate on! Keep it on....God is your covering. Sleep in it, eat in it, pray in it, rejoice in it and cry in it. As the Apostle Paul said in the book of Roman 8:35-39, *I'll let nothing separate me from the love of GOD.* Ephesians 6:10 - *Finally, my brethren, be strong in the Lord, and in the power of his might.* Ephesians 6:11- *Put on the whole armor of God that ye may be able to stand against the wiles of the devil.* Ephesians 6:13 - *Wherefore take unto you the whole armor of God, that ye may be able to withstand in the evil day, and having done all, to stand.* Ephesians 6:14 - *Stand therefore, having your loins girt about with truth, and having on the breastplate of righteousness.*

Bishop Randy and Evangelist Louise Cheatham

Breastplate of Judgment
(English Translation)

8

INTRODUCTION

On the fourth Sunday of June 2004, as I was slain in the Spirit, prostrate on the floor of my church, I remember God speaking to me amongst other things about the BREASTPLATE that the High Priest wore in the Old Testament. I had come across it in earlier readings; however, I had not paid close attention to the text found in the book of Exodus. *He showed me the BREASTPLATE in a vision as I had my eyes closed with the different colored stones.* I only remember getting up from my bed (floor) and thinking that I must research the importance of this BREASTPLATE. The significance was not apparent at the time.

This book details some of what I learned from the Throne Room of God!

Never underestimate the movement or the power of Holy Spirit, His gentle touch. Do not resist Him. In His presence, we are forever changed. He is able and will "download" His treasures from heaven and share His secrets. As believers in Christ, let's labor to spend time with Him — Our God so enjoys His children and longs to be with us. I am awestruck by His wonders especially as described by the book of Job.

He is able and will "download" His treasures from heaven and share His secrets.

9

1

THE PURPOSE

For by Him all things were created that are in heaven and that are on earth, visible and invisible, whether thrones or dominions or principalities or powers. All things were created through Him and for Him. And He is before all things, and in Him all things consist. And He is head of the body, the church, who is the beginning, the firstborn from the dead, that in all things He may have pre-eminence. (Colossians 1:16-18)

Another name for the BREASTPLATE that Aaron wore was the 'breastplate of judgment'. This is described in Exodus 28 & 39 as part of the priestly garment given to Moses by God. It was so because of the role of the high priest — to give atonement for the sins of the people and himself. It served as a covering and rested on the top of the ephod

ಬಲ

It was at this place of mercy that the high priest bore the judgment of the children of Israel upon his heart (Exodus 28:29).

ಬಲ

garment as he stood in the gap and entered into God's presence in the Holy of Holies. It was at this place of mercy that the high priest bore the judgment of the children of Israel upon his heart (Exodus 28:29). The implication was that God held this one man Aaron in a place of authority and accountability for His people. He and his sons were consecrated or set apart to minister unto the Lord (Exodus 28:3).

The BREASTPLATE contained twelve stones representing the tribes of Israel.

11

The BREASTPLATE and the other holy garments were special and only Aaron could wear them in order to minister in the high priest's office. Even the very garments of Aaron spoke of worship, honor, praise and thanksgiving. For that is the way the people of God must present themselves before entering His presence.

Even the very garments of Aaron spoke of worship, honor, praise and thanksgiving.

The holy garments were for glory and for beauty (Exodus 28:2). Then the beauty was symbolic of quality of excellence in all we do as unto Him. It gives pleasure to Him.

Continuing with construction of the BREASTPLATE; it was composed of two pieces of cloth (9x9") sewn together to create a pouch (Exodus 28:16). Inside the pouch was kept the Urim and Thummim which God commanded the high priest to use to determine God's will (Exodus 28:30 & Leviticus 8:8 & Numbers 27:18-21). It was believed that they were two stones or objects of different color or composition to distinguish between a 'yes' or 'no' given by God. The actual translation in Hebrew for the two names are: lights and perfections. We know that light is the medium for vision in order to see or to know. Perfection is symbolic of flawlessness, without blemish, and soundness. This was the means by which God chose to communicate His will to the high priest and thereby His people. Not much is described in the scriptures as to how the objects were used and what they looked like.

Inside the pouch was kept the Urim and Thummim which God commanded the high priest to use to determine God's will (Exodus 28:30 & Leviticus 8:8 & Numbers 27:18-21).

12

2

SIGNIFICANCE OF THE STONES

On the BREASTPLATE, each individual tribal name represented all members of his entire family — as is typical of the father or patriarch of the household. God was continuously reminded of the need for mercy — extended to the people.

There is no mention in the scriptures of the specific tribe for each unique stone.

The stones were listed in order with four rows of the three settings of stones, according to Exodus 28:17-20. The Hebrew method of writing was from left to right; therefore, the engravings of the stones were placed in that order from left to right. There is no mention in the scriptures of the specific tribe for each unique stone.

It is stated by God in Exodus 28:21:

> *"And the stones shall be with the names of the children of Israel, twelve, according to their names…"*

It was also stated earlier in the chapter that the names of the tribes would be inscribed on two onyx stones on the shoulders of the ephod — six on one and six on the other, according to the birth date of Israel's (Jacob's) sons (Exodus 28:10). To this point, God was using another means other than chronological birthdates to disclose the placement of the names in the BREASTPLATE.

There are three for which God gave the revelation right away — I am confident in terms of the order.

The first stone is Sardius, which is dark red in color, representing the blood and the lineage of Jesus and is inscribed with the tribe of Judah. Jesus is said to be the Lion of Judah. He purchased us with His own blood (Romans 5:8-9). He is also described as the "*first and the last,*" or Alpha and Omega (beginning and end).

The twelfth stone represents the youngest or the last son of Israel and is inscribed with tribe of Benjamin. Benjamin's name means "son of my right hand." This stone is the Jasper, which is clear/transparent. Revelation 4:3 states… *"he who sat (on the throne) was to be looked upon like a jasper and sardine (sardius) stone."* When Jesus cleansed us from sin, He washed us white as snow (Isaiah 1:18).

The second stone is Topaz and is inscribed with the tribe of Reuben. In the natural sense, he was the firstborn of Israel. His name signified "behold a son." Collectively, all the stones have tribal names with meanings that represent or tell the story of Jesus– one stone upon another. I received the balance of the order of the tribal names subsequently over time after continuing to seek Holy Spirit for revelation and began to capture on record. (See Chapter 4 and the Breastplate diagram, page 8)

Collectively, all the stones have tribal names with meanings that represent or tell the story of Jesus– one stone upon another.

2
PERSONAL REFLECTION & NOTES

2

PERSONAL REFLECTION & NOTES

3

OLD TESTAMENT CONCEALED NEW TESTAMENT REVEALED

In a similar manner today in the new dispensation, we see a relationship between Jesus and the BREASTPLATE that the High Priest wore in the Old Testament:

(1) Jesus is our High Priest who is also the spotless Lamb of God that was slain before the foundation of the world. He was the perfect sacrifice and blameless, without sin. He forever intercedes for us in heaven. As the high priest did for the nation of Israel, Jesus does for us today, and because He gave himself as a sacrifice; there is no need for continuous blood sacrifices. His blood redeemed all

Jesus is our High Priest who is also the spotless Lamb of God that was slain before the foundation of the world.

mankind once and for all within the Holy of Holies upon the mercy seat in heaven. The high priest covered the sins of himself and the people with the blood of animals, but Jesus bore our sins on the cross and removed the stain of our sins, as if it never occurred.

(2) Jesus' promise of the Comforter or Holy Spirit would make it possible to know the will of God without the Urim and Thummim. Because of His death, burial and resurrection from the dead, He

accomplished His work in the earth, after which, He said it was expedient that he leave so that he could send the Comforter. The Comforter who is the 3rd person of the Trinity is Holy Spirit and comes to live in our hearts. The gospel of John recorded Jesus words that amongst several actions of the Spirit, He would lead us into all truth. In other words provide the necessary guidance that we need to live this life and please the Father. (John 16:7, 13) In the Old Testament, Jeremiah the prophet prophesied of the days we are living in which God would…

The gospel of John recorded Jesus words that amongst several actions of the Spirit, He would lead us into all truth.

'put my law in their inward parts, and write it in their hearts: and I will be their God, and they shall be my people.' (Jer. 31:33)

(3) Jesus covers us just as a BREASTPLATE covered the high priests. The BREASTPLATE was for the purpose of covering the heart – the source of life for the body. The heart of a man in scripture represents the hidden or inner man – the spirit of the man. It is the inner man that requires protection (covering) by Christ. Our lives are hidden with Christ in God. (Colossians. 3:3). He is our life. WE are to 'put on Christ' according to Galatians 3:27. Additionally, Paul states in Ephesians 6:14 *'Stand therefore…and having on the BREASTPLATE of righteousness'* in describing a piece of the whole armor of God that we put on. Guess what!!! – Jesus is the righteousness of God (Hebrews 10:10-12, 19-21; 2 Corinthians 5:21). He is also described by the Prophet Jeremiah: *'Now this is His name by which He will be called: The Lord Our Righteousness.'* .

The heart of a man in scripture represents the hidden or inner man – the spirit of the man.

18

The Garments of the High Priest
(Exodus 28:4-43)

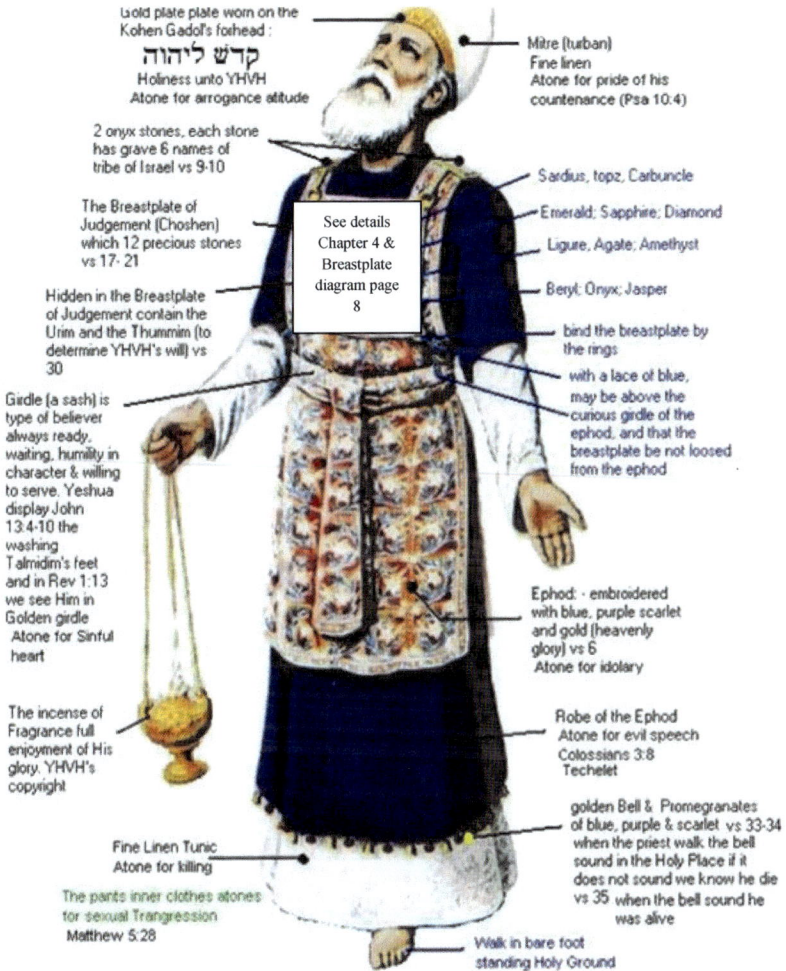

Gold plate plate worn on the Kohen Gadol's forhead :

קדש ליהוה

Holiness unto YHVH
Atone for arrogance attitude

Mitre (turban)
Fine linen
Atone for pride of his countenance (Psa 10:4)

2 onyx stones, each stone has grave 6 names of tribe of Israel vs 9-10

The Breastplate of Judgement (Choshen) which 12 precious stones vs 17- 21

Hidden in the Breastplate of Judgement contain the Urim and the Thummim (to determine YHVH's will) vs 30

Girdle (a sash) is type of believer always ready, waiting, humility in character & willing to serve. Yeshua display John 13:4-10 the washing Talmidim's feet and in Rev 1:13 we see Him in Golden girdle Atone for Sinful heart

The incense of Fragrance full enjoyment of His glory. YHVH's copyright

Sardius, topz, Carbuncle
Emerald; Sapphire; Diamond
Ligure, Agate; Amethyst
Beryl: Onyx; Jasper

bind the breastplate by the rings

with a lace of blue, may be above the curious girdle of the ephod, and that the breastplate be not loosed from the ephod

See details Chapter 4 & Breastplate diagram page 8

Ephod: - embroidered with blue, purple scarlet and gold (heavenly glory) vs 6
Atone for idolary

Robe of the Ephod
Atone for evil speech
Colossians 3:8
Techelet

golden Bell & Promegranates of blue, purple & scarlet vs 33-34 when the priest walk the bell sound in the Holy Place if it does not sound we know he die vs 35 when the bell sound he was alive

Fine Linen Tunic
Atone for killing

The pants inner clothes atones for sexual Trangression
Matthew 5:28

Walk in bare foot standing Holy Ground

Priestly Garment with Breastplate
(www.gorepent.com 2010)

19

3
PERSONAL REFLECTION & NOTES

_____

_____

_____

_____

_____

_____

_____

_____

_____

_____

_____

_____

_____

_____

_____

_____

_____

_____

_____

_____

_____

_____

_____

_____

_____

_____

_____

_____

_____

3

PERSONAL REFLECTION & NOTES

_____
_____
_____
_____
_____
_____
_____
_____
_____
_____
_____
_____
_____
_____
_____
_____
_____
_____
_____
_____
_____
_____
_____
_____
_____
_____

JESUS' STORY

CHILD	Judah Jehovah to be praised	BIRTH
	Reuben Behold a Son	
	Issachar Came as a servant	
MAN	Simeon Hearing/Discernment	MINISTRY
	Levi Joined	
	Zebulun Dwelling	
SACRIFICIAL LAMB	Asher Happy/ Blessed	ROAD OF SUFFERING
	Naphtali Wrestling in Blessing	
	Dan Judgment Ministered	
KING	Gad Troop/Breakthrough	VICTOR
	Joseph Bountiful/Increaser	
	Benjamin Son of my Right Hand	

4

THE STONES TELL THE STORY OF JESUS

The STORY of Jesus is told through the meaning of the names of the tribes of Israel on the breastplate of judgment.

Jesus was in the beginning with Jehovah (Father) God as the Word —— part of the Godhead or second person of the Trinity as the SON.

He came through the tribe of Judah born to a virgin named Mary. His was a supernatural birth which God used as a "sign" for the nation of Israel. His earthly father was Joseph. There were 42 generations through which Jesus came as recorded in the Gospel of Matthew. His purpose was predestined by His Father to "*save his people from their sins*" and they called his name "Emmanuel" which means 'God with us.' His title, which is sometimes mistaken for His last name, is "Christ," the Greek word for "Savior" or "Messiah" — another expression is **Jehovah God OUR Salvation**. In the Old Testament, the tribe of Judah — meaning **"praise"** — would go first and lead the other tribes when the nation would go out for battle.

His birth was prophesied by the Prophet Isaiah 700+ years before

His purpose was predestined by His Father to "save his people from sin" and they called his name "Emmanuel" which means 'God with us'.

He came to the earth as a baby and **Son of God.** He became flesh in order to live life as a man and to set our example. It was also given to the prophet the location of the birth, which was Bethlehem. The angels announced to the shepherds in the field on the night of his birth that the Christ child was born in the city of David in a stable. The first carriers of the good news of the gospel were the shepherds who spread the word around the surrounding area. As the news reached King Herod, he attempted to locate Jesus because he was threatened by the prophetic word that Jesus was destined to be ruler and king over Israel. He wanted to destroy Him and even attempted to do so! Of course, God made provision for Jesus as a child so that no harm came to Him. His earthly father Joseph was warned in a dream by an angel to flee to Egypt with his family. He later returned to Judea and lived in a city called Nazareth after the death of King Herod.

As a son, He grew, and He **served** his Father, his earthly parents, and the chosen people. In the gospel account by Luke (the great physician and disciple), we find Jesus, at the age of twelve, listening and asking questions in the temple among the scholars/teachers. When Joseph and Mary find Him, after leaving and then returning back to Jerusalem to locate Him (they erroneously had assumed He was amongst the traveling caravan), He tells them, "Did you not know that I must be about my Father's business?" In the epistle to the Philippians, the Apostle Paul describes Jesus as "*one who made*

As the news reached King Herod, he attempted to locate Jesus because he was threatened by the prophetic word that Jesus was destined to be ruler and king over Israel.

In the epistle to the Philippians, the Apostle Paul describes Jesus as "one who made Himself of no reputation but took on the form of a servant and was made in the likeness of men."

Himself of no reputation but took on the form of a servant and was made in the likeness of men." In many passages in the bible, Jesus demonstrates servant-hood. He is the perfect example of all that He represented when He came to live as a man. He announced in the book of Luke that He came to "seek and save the lost" as He encountered religious leaders who criticized Him for dining with

෨෨෬෮

He told the disciples that the greatest in the kingdom would be the ones with the servant heart.

෨෨෬෮

the chief publican, Zacchaeus, as He was traveling through Jericho. He told the disciples that the greatest in the kingdom would be the ones with the servant heart. At the last supper, just before His crucifixion, He washed the disciples' feet as an example that they should likewise be willing to wash one another's feet.

He is authenticated by His Father through the forerunner John the Baptist at the River Jordan when He is baptized as a man. His Father opens the heavens and the Holy Spirit lightning upon Jesus like a dove with an audible voice that said He was the Son and God was pleased with Him. Jesus **heard** His marching orders to begin His ministry at the age of 30, which began with being tempted by Satan, the devil, for forty days in the wilderness as He fasted and prayed. When the devil was unable to tempt Jesus to operate independently of His Father, He departed from Him for a season. Luke 4:14 states:

෨෨෬෮

His Father opens the heavens and the Holy Spirit lightning upon Jesus like a dove with an audible voice that said he was the Son and God was pleased with Him.

෨෨෬෮

"And Jesus returned in the power of the Spirit into Galilee: and there went out a fame of him through all the region round about."

He immediately **joined** himself to twelve men whom He sought out as disciles to teach and train about the Kingdom of God and His purpose for coming: to die for the sins of man. The twelve were referred to as "apostles" of the church: Simon Peter and Andrew (brothers), James and John (brothers and sons of Zebedee), Philip, Bartholomew, Thomas, Matthew (tax collector) James (son of Alphaeus, Thaddaeus, Simon (the Canaanite) and Judas Iscariot (the betrayer). They functioned as Christ's servants on earth who healed the sick/diseased, delivered people, fed the hungry and basically performed the works that Jesus did. The relationship of Jesus and His disciples grew close and intimate. Much power was demonstrated as they trusted His teaching and were obedient to His commands. They began to

He understood each one-their strengths and weaknesses; nevertheless He loved and entrusted them with the building of the church (Greek= ekklesia).

understand His authority and that he was truly the Son of God. He understood each one-their strengths and weaknesses; nevertheless He loved and entrusted them with the building of the *church* (Greek= ekklesia). Eventually, He came to a place that he shared the plan of God — that three days after His death/crucifixion, He would be resurrected through the power of Holy Spirit from the dead to defeat death (separation), hell (consequences of sin) and the grave (permanency). He also assured them that though they would be saddened by His death, there would be great joy at His appearing — much like a mother who travails to bring forth a child and the joy she experiences. At the same time, the Comforter Holy Spirit would take up residence in the hearts (of men) and in the earth after Jesus' return to the Father. He told of going to the Father to prepare a place for them and all the children of God where we would be forever with Him and reign in the new heaven and new earth!

As Jesus introduced the Kingdom to the nation of Israel, a new covenant was introduced through the New Testament. In this covenant, instead of the keeping of the law (Ten Commandments) housed in the Ark of the Covenant in the Holy of Holies in the tabernacle, he wrote the law upon their

In the New Testament, the book of Hebrews speaks of a "true tabernacle" as a place not made with hands.

the law upon their hearts. So our hearts became the tabernacle of **His dwelling (place)**. In the Old Testament, the high priest would go into the Holy of Holies and place the blood of animals upon the mercy seat of the Ark of the Covenant once per year, to make atonement for his sins, his family, and the sins of the people. The Ark was originally carried in a tent; however, later, it was placed into the temple that King Solomon constructed at the direction of his father, King David, before he died. In the New Testament, the book of Hebrews speaks of a "true tabernacle" as a place not made with hands. Also Revelations 21:3 states:

ଛଠଔଓ

At the age of 33, Jesus concluded His earthly assignment after spending and investing much time, teaching the twelve disciples as well as many others who joined Him.

ଛଠଔଓ

> "Behold, the tabernacle of God is with man, and He will **dwell** with them, and they shall be his people…"

At the age of 33, Jesus concluded His earthly assignment after spending and investing much time, teaching the twelve disciples as well as many others who joined Him. As a side note, many women followed Jesus and also "funded" his ministry. He was **blessed** by the Father and released to return to heaven after establishing the kingdom of God on earth, beginning with the 120 disciples, later baptized with the Holy Ghost in the Upper Room as instructed by Jesus before His ascension. He prayed to the Father, announcing that…

> "…while I was with them in the world, I kept them in Your name. Those whom you gave Me I have kept, and none of them is lost except the son of perdition, that the Scripture might be fulfilled. But I come to You, and these things I speak in the world, that they may have My joy fulfilled in themselves." (John 17:12-13)

In another account during His ministry, Jesus addressed the crowd in the city of Capernaum that followed Him and the disciples in masses after the miraculous feeding of the 5000 men, (not including women and children):

"All that the Father giveth me shall come to me, and him that cometh to me I will in no wise cast out. For I came down from heaven, not to do mine own will, but the will of him who sent me. And this is the Father's will which hath sent me, that of all which he hath given me I should lose nothing, but should raise it up again at the last day." (John 6:37-40)

Just before going to the cross and His crucifixion for remitting (remission of our sins through the shedding of His blood) our punishment, it was necessary for Jesus to go to the place of crushing or pressing called the Garden of Gethsemane (olive press). It was a place believed to have had a press for crushing olives because it was in the midst of an olive grove. This occurred right after the Last Supper, very early in the morning, with His disciples, where He announced that one of the twelve would betray Him willfully. The garden was a place of sorrow and agony. It was a place where Jesus had to reckon

ഐൽൃ

It was a place where Jesus had to reckon with enduring separation for the first time ever from the Father and severe suffering of on the cross, as He would be nailed hands and feet to the cross.

ഐൽൃ

with enduring separation for the first time ever from the Father and severe suffering of on the cross, as He would be nailed hands and feet to the cross.

The Roman crucifixion was deemed as the worst type of punishment and torture because an individual's flesh was torn, bones pierced, and joints separated as the person hung. From a natural standpoint, to breathe, the body would attempt to rise up just so that the lungs could expand. Ultimately the person died of exhaustion or asphyxiation.

ഐൽൃ

Jesus overcame His "soulish man" and persevered through significant anguish as He yielded Himself for the sake of all mankind and the Father's will!

ഐൽൃ

Even though the entire group went with Jesus to the garden, it was the three disciples closest to Jesus — Peter, James and John — who further escorted Him into the garden to pray. He specifically asked them to watch, be alert, and pray for Him because of what He was facing. Unfortunately, He found them asleep after three attempts. The scripture says that he agonized so much so that His sweat became great drops of blood — symbolizing the body in extreme anguish. Jesus **wrestled in blessing** because He said to the Father during His personal prayer time in the garden according to Luke 22:42, *"Father, if it is your will, take this cup away from Me; nevertheless not My will, but Yours, be done."* Jesus overcame His "soulish man" and perseveres through significant anguish as He yielded Himself for the sake of all mankind and the Father's will!

He knew that they were actually envious of Jesus and His popularity, which could threaten their position in the Jewish community.

In his sentencing of Jesus to the cross, the governor Pontius Pilate of the Roman government recognized that Jesus was not guilty of any wrongdoing or that He had broken any of the Roman laws worthy of death; however, he thought that by severely scourging or beating Jesus unmercifully to the point of being close to death, the chief high priest and the political and religious leaders would be satisfied. He knew that they were actually envious of Jesus and His popularity, which could threaten their position in the Jewish community. During the Passover, also called the Feast of Unleavened Bread — the first major celebration during the Jewish year and a major holiday — it was customary that a prisoner could be pardon or released. The Passover was a time of commemoration of the time that the Jews prepared for the exodus out of Egypt (in haste) to the promised land of Canaan led by the Prophet Moses. The Pharisees knew the scripture spoke of the Christ or Messiah who would come and "usher in a kingdom of peace and prosperity," and since they knew the Romans were not concern about Pharisaical laws concerning blasphemy (irreverence by equating oneself to God), they perverted the message by saying that Jesus opposed Caesar Tiberius (the Roman emperor) by agreeing that He was King of the Jews. They convinced the mob of people to crucify Jesus and release the murderer named Barnabas, who was sentenced to die.

As Jesus was dying, the soldiers and Pharisees made mockery of Him as He hung naked on the cross and derided Him by commenting that, if He was able to save others, He should be able to save Himself. To add insult to injury, they placed the cross high on a place called Golgotha (place of the skull) near the city in view of many passing by. Pontius Pilate placed a sign above His head in Greek, Latin, and Hebrew with the writing "JESUS OF NAZARETH, THE KING OF THE JEWS."

ॐ

Because Jesus willfully died and did so without committing sin, He served as the high priest, and, as the sacrificial lamb, His blood was (is) payment in full.

ॐ

It is noteworthy that the Passover Feast occurred during the same time as Jesus' death. As instructed by Moses in the Old Testament, the doorpost above the entrance and side posts of the Israelites' homes was smeared with the blood of a lamb sacrificed and eaten the night before the exodus out of Egypt. Because of the hardness of Pharaoh's heart, and unbeknownst to him he pronounced a judgment of death over his entire country and people affecting the first-born sons, including the animals. Hence, all those who had the blood applied, the death angel passed over — no exceptions. God's requirement for sin was sacrificing of animals, because without the blood, there was no remission for sins. The high priest had to sacrifice not only for the people, but also for Himself.

ॐ

Because of Jesus we are made free — free from addictions, sinful habits, an evil conscience, and so much more.

ॐ

Because Jesus willfully died and did so without committing sin, He served as the High Priest, and, as the sacrificial lamb, His blood was (is) payment in full. It was the only blood acceptable to God under the new covenant:

"But Christ came as High Priest of the good things to come, with the greater and more perfect tabernacle not made with hands, that is, not of this creation. Not with the blood of goats and calves, but with His own blood He entered the Most Holy Place once for all, having obtained eternal redemption. For if the blood of bulls and goats and the ashes of a heifer, sprinkling the unclean, sanctifies for

the purifying of the flesh, how much more shall the blood of Christ, who through the eternal Spirit offered Himself without spot to God, cleanse your conscience from dead works to serve the living God?" (Heb 9:11-14)

The cross has been a major stumbling block in the way of the Jews, preventing the majority of them from accepting Jesus, as Messiah. The Apostle Paul summed up the importance of the crucifixion best: "We preach Christ crucified, to the Jews a stumbling block and to the Greeks foolishness, but to those who are called, both Jews and Greeks, Christ the power of God and the wisdom of God" (1 Corinthians 1:23-24). Out of the ugliness and agony of the crucifixion, God accomplished the greatest good of all– the redemption of sinners.

- Nelson's New English Bible Dictionary

Judgment was ministered for all mankind ONCE AND FOR ALL. The last words of Jesus before releasing His spirit to Father God were "It is finished"! His work was complete and final.

Psalms 18:29 states: *"For by You I can run through a **troop**, by my God I can leap over a wall."* Jesus overcame death, hell and the grave as a result of the sacrificial offering of Himself for the sins of the whole world. He laid down his life and **broke through** to the enemy's (Satan) camp when He was resurrected from the dead after three days in the grave through the power of Holy Spirit. All authority and power was given to Him. His life became a ransom for our lives. When a sinner comes to Jesus and asks for forgiveness, an exchange takes place. Satan, called the "prince of this age," loses legal authority and control over the born-again believer. Jesus deposits His authority through Holy Spirit. We become Spirit-led versus a life of being subject to sin and the curse of the law! Because of Jesus we are made free — free from addictions, sinful habits, an evil

Satan was a high-ranking angel (cherub) in heaven named Lucifer- meaning "light bearer".

conscience, and so much more. The book of Hebrews gives us a glimpse of Jesus' motivation of love:

> *"Jesus, the author and finisher of our faith; who for the joy that was set before him endured the cross, despising the shame, and is set down at the right hand of the throne of God ." (Hebrews 12:2)*

ℰℭ

His desire is to vindicate himself by causing as many men, women, boys, and girls to reject God by rejecting His Son.

ℰℭ

Our 'Daddy God' desired a relationship with us as His children, and, by removing the barrier of sin, Jesus became our righteousness and established fellowship once again that was lost by Adam in Genesis. Everyone born in the earth is subject to a life of slavery to sin and destined for hell (excluding babies and little ones not yet at the age of accountability) in torment and apart from the Father forever and all eternity. How wonderful the plan of God is, that He sent His only Son that we could have the gift of eternal life.

The place called hell was established for Satan, the devil, and the one-third of heaven's angels that followed him in rebellion against God. Satan was a high-ranking angel (cherub) in heaven named Lucifer- meaning "light bearer".

He was beautiful, and his original physical form/appearance is described in Ezekiel 28:13:

> *Thou hast been in Eden the garden of God; every precious stone [was] thy covering, the sardius, topaz, and the diamond, the beryl, the onyx, and the jasper, the sapphire, the emerald, and the carbuncle, and gold: the workmanship of thy tabrets and of thy pipes was prepared in thee in the day that thou wast created.*

Based on the scriptures, it has been inferred that he made music with his physical movements and may have been the "worship leader" in heaven. He was expelled from heaven along with the others, came to earth and was responsible for tempting Eve in disobeying God and then Adam, her husband. His mission in the earth has been since the beginning to kill, steal and destroy. His desire is to vindicate himself by causing as many men, women, boys, and girls to reject God by rejecting His Son. He's awaiting his final destination, referred to as "the lake of fire" in Revelation 19 and 20, and he wants company. Such a sweet victory Jesus wrought in defeating Satan at the cross. He knew the plan from the beginning — born to die, but with such a precious outcome. HE GOT UP!!!!!

"….Death is swallowed up in victory. O death, Where is thy sting? O grave, where is thy victory? The sting of death is sin; and the strength of sin is the law. But thanks be to God, which giveth us the victory through our Lord Jesus Christ."
(I Corinthians 15:55-57)

ഇൗരു

Jesus is our example and because He showed us the way to victory by doing only what He saw the Father do and saying only what He heard the Father say, in obedience, we are able to do likewise.

ഇൗരു

In the book of Acts, after Jesus' ascension to the heavens and the disciples' baptism in the Holy Spirit on the day of Pentecost (which occurred fifty days after the Passover), the Apostle Peter boldly preaches to the audience of devout Jews out of every nation…

"Ye men of Israel, hear these words; Jesus of Nazareth, a man approved of God among you by miracles and wonders and signs, which God did by him in the midst of your counsel, as ye yourselves also know: Him, being delivered by the determinate counsel and foreknowledge of God, ye have taken, and by wicked hands crucified and slain: Whom God hath raised up, having loosed the pains of death: because it was not possible that he should be holden of it."
(Acts 2:22-24)

Jesus is our example and because He showed us the way to victory by doing only what He saw the Father do and saying only what He heard the Father say, in obedience, we are able to do likewise. Jesus is described as the Lamb of God that overcame Satan in the book of Revelations. The Apostle Paul, in multiple epistles or writings, tells us several times that we are able to live victorious lives because of what Jesus accomplished. One of the most-often quoted scriptures by preachers today comes from II Corinthians 2:14:

"Now thanks be unto God, which always causeth us to triumph in Christ, and maketh manifest the savour of his knowledge by us in every place."

John 1:12 states, *"For as many as received him, to them gave He power to become the sons of God, even to them that believe on His name."* So many sons (and daughters) have entered the kingdom of God because of the work of Jesus Christ. Much like He used the parable in teaching the disciples about a seed first having to die, being planted into the ground. What happens? A miracle begins in the ground; the multiplication of the single seed and then many more to follow. That's what occurred

Much like He used the parable in teaching the disciples about a seed first having to die, being planted into the ground.

— a **bountiful** harvest and a significant **increase** in the family of God. Jesus is that seed that was planted. We are as jewels in the crown of Jesus, the King of Kings and Lord of Lords. He has the awesome privilege of presenting us as a chaste bride at the marriage supper to Our Father.

In His place of authority, Jesus took His seat as the **Son of my right hand** next to the Father in glory after His return to heaven and presenting His blood on the mercy seat of the ark. He is ever interceding for us as Elder brother and High Priest in heaven. As stated earlier, the Apostle Peter addresses the Jewish congregants during the Day of Pentecost with the following exhortation:

He is ever interceding for us as Elder brother and High Priest in heaven.

"This Jesus hath God raised up, whereof we are all witnesses. Therefore being by the right Hand of God exalted, and having received of the Father the promise of the Holy Ghost, he hath shed forth this, which ye now see and hear. For David is not ascended into the heavens: but he saith himself, 'The Lord said unto my Lord, Sit thou on my right hand, until I make thy foes thy footstool.' Therefore let all the house of Israel know assuredly, that God hath made that same Jesus, whom ye have crucified, both Lord and Christ." (Acts 2:32-36)

4

PERSONAL REFLECTION & NOTES

4

PERSONAL REFLECTION & NOTES

_____
_____
_____
_____
_____
_____
_____
_____
_____
_____
_____
_____
_____
_____
_____
_____
_____
_____
_____
_____
_____
_____
_____
_____
_____
_____
_____
_____

5
PHOTO GALLERY

Shepherds on hillside of Bethlehem

Overview of city of David– Jerusalem
Holy City

Author, baptism in River Jordan– Israel
Jesus baptized by Prophet John the Baptist

Sea of Galilee—Israel
Jesus taught twelve disciples

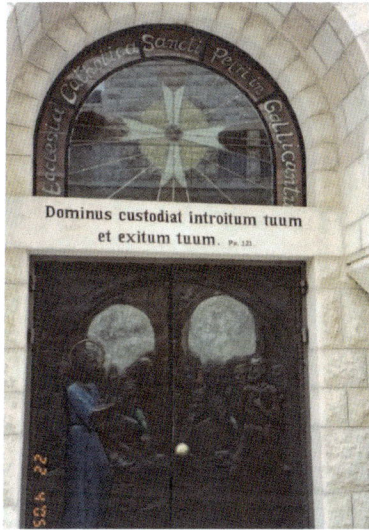

Door of St. Peter's church– Israel
Jesus with twelve disciples

Model of Solomon's Temple (wall around old city of Jerusalem)
Holy of Holies depicted with arrow

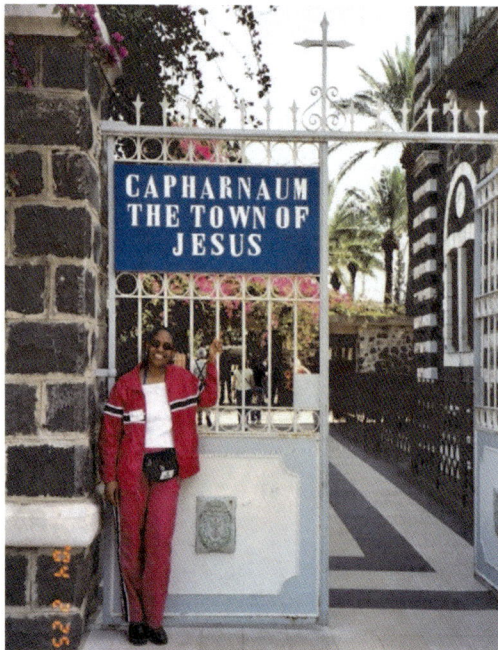

Author @ entrance into Capernaum- Israel
Jesus addressed massive crowds in town

Garden of Gethsemane– Israel
Jesus prayed before His crucifixion

Memorial plaque at the Garden of Gethsemane- Israel

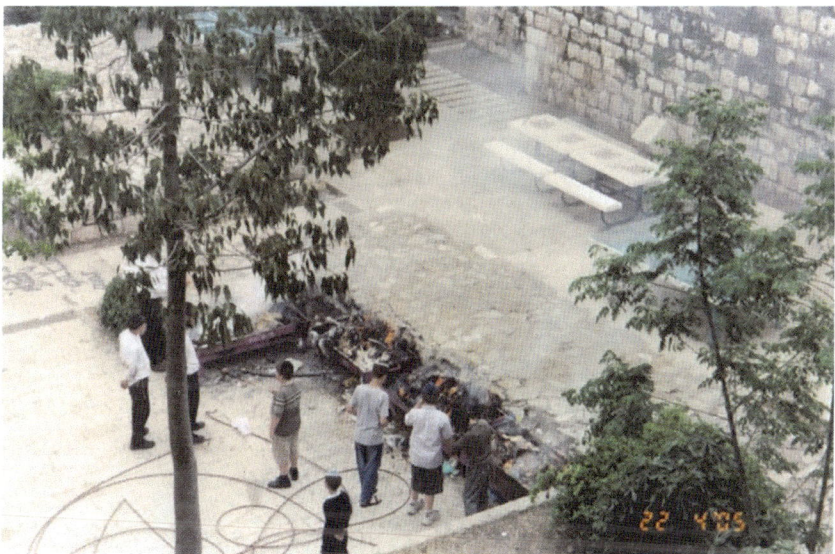

Preparation for Passover– burning of leaven– Israel
Jesus was the Passover Lamb

Road to Golgotha in Jerusalem
Jesus was led by Roman soldiers to cross

Golgotha (Place of the skull)- Jerusalem
Jesus crucified on the cross

Memorial of Apostle Peter– Israel
One of Jesus' "inner circle" disciples

Entrance to Garden Tomb– Israel
Jesus' burial place

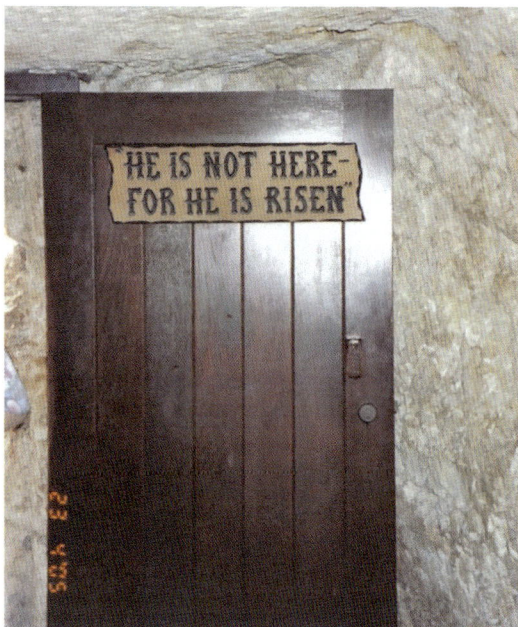

Door leading to empty tomb– Israel
Jesus rose from the dead

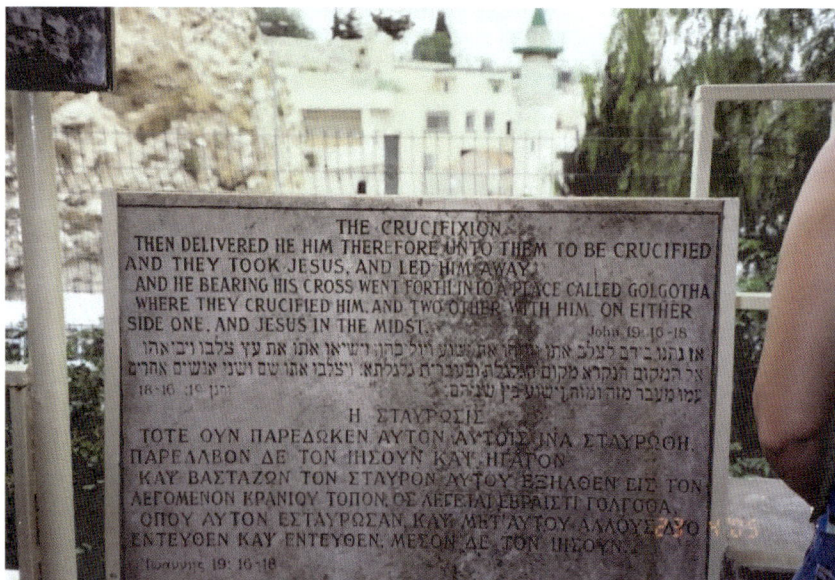

Memorial plaque of crucifixion @ Golgotha site
Jesus was crucified to a cross

Mount of Olives (world's largest Jewish cemetery) – Israel
Jesus will land on the site upon His return

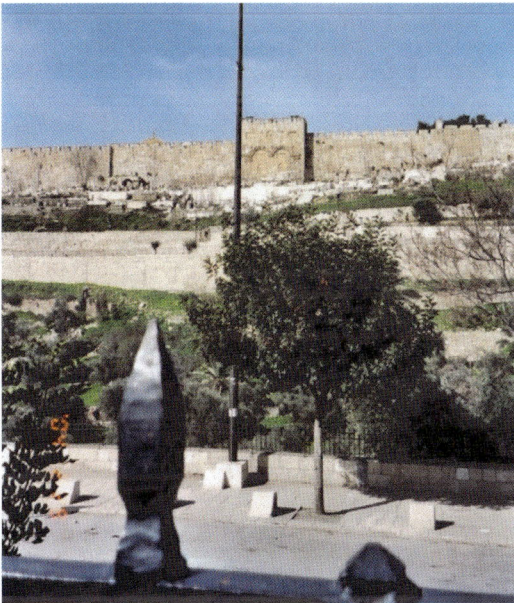

Eastern Gate (also called Golden Gate)- Old city of Jerusalem
Historians say Jesus will enter upon His return
(biblical reference in Ezekiel)

6

MORE ON THE STONES IN THE BIBLE

The stone in the Word of God represents either a holy or precious person or a "thing" that is significant to our God. A stone is, defined by Webster's dictionary as a hard or compacted material or earthly matter: rock. It is difficult to break or alter. The stone typifies a type of covenant.

In the Old Testament, God writes the Ten Commandments on two tablets of stones (both sides) for the Prophet Moses to instruct the nation of Israel after the exodus out of Egypt, en route to the promised land of Canaan. The commandments were given so that the chosen people understood what was acceptable and likewise unacceptable to God. Moses received the tablets twice as a result of destroying the first set when he threw it at the people after learning of their riotous sinful behavior and participation in serious idolatry. They became impatient while he "delayed" on the top of Mount Sinai with God.

"When I was gone up into the mount to receive the tablets of stone, even the tables of the covenant which the Lord made with you, then I abode in the mount forty day and forty nights, I neither did eat bread nor drink water. And the Lord delivered unto me two tablets of stone written with the finger of God; and on them was written according to all the words, which the Lord spake with you

in the mount out of the midst of the fire in the day of assembly. And it came to pass at the end of forty days and forty nights, that the Lord gave me the two tablets of stone, even the tables of the covenant. And the Lord said unto me, Arise, get thee own hence; for thy people which thou has brought forth out of Egypt have corrupted themselves; they are quickly turned aside out of the way which I commanded them; they have made them a molten image."
(Deuteronomy 9: 9-12)

Additionally, as Moses and the other patriarchs of the bible were commanded by God, they "hewed" (cut) altars out of stone when making blood sacrifices as they traveled and lodged in various places. When an event of significant proportions occurred in a location, the man of God would make a memorial of stone and leave it in place as a "marker." As an example, in the book of Joshua 24: 24-27:

"And the people said unto Joshua, 'The Lord our God we will serve and his voice will we obey.' So Joshua made a covenant with the people that day, and set them a statue and an ordinance in Shechem. And Joshua wrote there words in the book of the law of God, and took a great stone, and set it up there under an oak, that was by the sanctuary of the Lord. And Joshua said unto all the people, 'Behold, this stone shall be a witness unto us; for it hath heard all the words of the Lord which he spake unto us: it shall be therefore a witness unto you, lest ye deny God."

Stones were used as a means of judgment per commandments given by God as part of the law in certain instances, such as: a woman caught in an adulterous act; a stubborn/rebellious son who consistently dishonored his parents even after chastening; an individual found serving and worshipping other gods, etc. The people of God — mainly the men — were required to "stone" the adult or child (of age) until they died. If the stoning occurred inside the camp (area of lodging), they removed their bodies because of the defilement of sin.

Jesus is described as the chief cornerstone of the spiritual building/ house of God and very precious.

"If so be ye have tasted that the Lord is gracious. To whom coming, as unto a living stone, disallowed indeed of men, but chosen of God, and precious…. Wherefore also it is contained in the scripture, Behold, I lay in Zion a chief cornerstone, elect, and precious: and he that believeth on him shall not be confounded… Unto you therefore which believe he is precious: but unto them which be disobedient, the stone which the builders disallowed, the same is made the head of the corner, and a stone of stumbling, and a rock of offence, even to them which stumble at the word, being disobedient: whereunto also they were appointed." (I Pet 2:3-4, 6-8)

In the book of Zechariah, the prophet speaks of "a stone with seven eyes" that foretells of Jesus prophetically. This description, very similar in nature, is also recorded by the Apostle John in Revelation 5:6:

"And I beheld, and lo, in the midst of the throne and of the four beasts, and in the midst of the elders, stood a lamb as it had been slain, having seven horns and seven eyes, which are the seven Spirits of God sent forth into all the earth."

The body of Christ is also called "lively and precious stones" making up the house, or the body of Christ.

"Ye also, as lively stones, are built up a spiritual house, an holy priesthood, to offer up spiritual sacrifices, acceptable to God by Jesus Christ. …But ye are a chosen generation, a royal priesthood, an holy nation, a peculiar people; that ye should show forth the praises of him who hath called you out of darkness into his marvelous light: which in times past were not a people, but are now the people of God: which had not obtained mercy, but now have obtained mercy."
(I Pet. 2:5, 9-10)

The little ones or children are referred to as "polished and precious stones." In the book of Lamentation, the prophet Jeremiah speaks concerning the mistreatment of the children as stones cast out of the sanctuary, with none that is concerned or willing to provide for them. They were once embraced as very valuable and worthy...

"How is the gold become dim! How is the most fine gold changed! The stones of the sanctuary are poured out in the top of every street. The precious sons of Zion, comparable to fine gold, how are they esteemed as earthen pitchers, the work of the hands of the potter! Even the sea monsters draw out the breast, they give suck to their young ones: the daughter of my people is become cruel, like the ostriches in the wilderness. The tongue of the suckling child cleaveth to the roof of his mouth for thirst: the young children ask bread, and no man breaketh it into them.... Her Nazarites were purer than snow, they were whiter than milk, they were more ruddy in body than rubies, their polishing was of sapphire: their visage is blacker than coal; they are not known in the streets; their skin cleaveth to their bones; it is withered, it is become like a stick." (Lam. 4:1-4, 7-8)

6

PERSONAL REFLECTION & NOTES

6

PERSONAL REFLECTION & NOTES

7

TRIBAL BLESSINGS BY ISRAEL
FATHER OF SONS

Israel was the grandson of Abraham, also known as the "father of faith" in scripture. We know from the Old Testament that God promised a goodly and godly heritage to Abraham and all of his descendants, including Jacob, whose name was changed to "Israel." Jacob returned to his homeland with his family and much wealth he amassed after years of separation from his twin brother Esau, whom he "swindled" out of his birthright by pretending to be him. Tradition holds that, before the father dies, he blesses his sons and specifically the firstborn with the special privilege of receiving the birthright. Jacob was able to convince their father Isaac, a man up in age, with difficulty seeing, that he was Esau, and, so, his father pronounced the blessing over Jacob. The night before Jacob meets Esau, he has an encounter with the "angel of the Lord" at a place called Peniel — east of the Jordan River. It was here that he received the blessing symbolized by the angel's pronouncement of a new name. Jacob had been known as a 'trickster' and 'deceiver' up to this point; however, through events with his uncle Laban and his vow to God at Bethel to eventually return to his kindred, he wanted to make things right between the two of them. So the book of Genesis records that he wrestled with the angel until the breaking of day:

"And when he saw that he prevailed not against Him, he touched the hollow of his thigh; and the hollow of Jacob's thigh was out of joint, as he wrestled with him. And he said, 'Let me go, for the day breaketh.' And he said, 'I will not let thee go, except thou bless me.' And he said unto him, 'What is thy name?' and he said, 'Jacob.' And he said, 'Thy name shall be called no more Jacob, but Israel: for as a prince hast thou power with God and with men, and hast prevailed." (Gen 32:25-28)

Israel was also the father of the twelve sons or tribes that were represented on the BREASTPLATE of judgment. Israel's wives were Leah and Rachel. He had children by the two handmaids as well, Zilpah and Bilhah. The sons of Leah were Reuben, Simeon, Levi, Judah, Issachar, and Zebulun. The sons of Rachel were Joseph and Benjamin. The sons of Zilpah were Gad and Asher. The sons of Bilhah were Dan and Naphtali. He had only one daughter, named Dinah, born after Leah's last son Zebulun.

On his deathbed, he gathered his sons and pronounced the blessing individually over each of them, recorded in the following verses of Genesis 49: 3-27:

Judah
Jehovah to Be Praised

"Judah, you are he whom your brothers shall praise; your hands shall be on the neck of your enemies; your father's children shall bow down before you.
Judah is a lion's whelp; from prey, my son, you have gone up. He bows down, he lies down as a lion; and as a lion, who shall rouse him?
The scepter shall not depart from Judah, nor a lawgiver from between his feet, until Shiloh comes; and to Him shall be the obedience of the people.
Binding his donkey to the vine, and his donkey's colt to the choice vine, he washed his garments in wine, and his clothes in the blood of grapes.
His eyes are darker than wine, and his teeth whiter than milk."

Reuben
Behold a Son

"Reuben, you are my firstborn, my might and the beginning of my strength, the excellency of dignity and the excellency of power. Unstable as water, you shall not excel, because you went up to your father's bed; then you defiled it — he went up to my couch."

Issachar
Came as a Servant

"Issachar is a strong donkey, lying down between two burdens; he saw that rest was good, and that the land was pleasant; he bowed his shoulder to bear a burden, and became a band of slaves."

Simeon and Levi
Hearing/Discernment — Joined

"Simeon and Levi are brothers; instruments of cruelty are in their dwelling place. Let not my soul enter their council; let honor be united to their assembly; for in their anger, they slew a man, and in their self-will they hamstrung an ox. Accursed be their anger, for it is fierce; and their wrath, for it is cruel! I will divide them in Jacob and scatter then in Israel."

Zebulun
Dwelling

"Zebulun shall dwell by the haven of the sea; he shall become a haven for ships, and his border shall adjoin Sidon."

Asher
Happy/Blessed

"Bread from Asher shall be rich, and he shall yield royal dainties."

Naphtali
Wrestling in Blessing

"Naphtali is a deer let loose; he uses beautiful words."

Dan
Judgment Ministered

"Dan shall judge his people as one of the tribes of Israel. Dan shall be a serpent by the way, a viper by the path that bites the horse's heel so that its rider shall fall backward. I have waited for your salvation O Lord!"

Gad
Troop/ Breakthrough

"Gad, a troop shall tramp upon him, but he shall triumph at last."

Joseph
Bountiful/Increaser

"Joseph is a fruitful bough, a fruitful bough by a well; his branches run over the wall. The archers have bitterly grieved him, shot at him and hated him. But his bow remained in strength, and the arms of his hands were made strong by the hands of the Mighty God of Jacob (from there is the Shepherd, the Stone of Israel), by the God of your father who will help you, and by the Almighty who will bless you with blessings of heaven above, blessings of the deep that lies beneath, blessings of the breasts and the womb. The blessings of your father have excelled the blessings of my ancestors, up to the utmost bound of the everlasting hills. They shall be on the head of Joseph, and on the crown of the head of him who was separate from his brothers."

Benjamin
Son of My Right Hand

"Benjamin is a ravenous wolf; in the morning he shall devour the prey, and at night he shall divide the spoil."

7
PERSONAL REFLECTION & NOTES

7
PERSONAL REFLECTION & NOTES

8

SUMMARY / PRAYER

"Hearken unto me, O house of Jacob, and all the remnant of the house of Israel, which are borne by me from the belly, which are carried from the womb: and even to your old age I am he; and even to hoar hairs will I carry you: I have made and I will bear; even I will carry, and will deliver you. To whom will ye liken me, and make me equal, and compare me, that we may be like?" (Isa. 46: 3-5)

Jesus referred to Himself when speaking to the Pharisees and Jewish religious leaders of the day as "I AM" when they questioned His authenticity as the Son of God. He is eternal. He was from the beginning with God the Father and Holy Spirit before the foundation of the world, and "is to come" in the future. He is scheduled at an appointed time to return to the earth for the body of Christ, or the church, to take us to our heavenly home. No one is like unto Him. It is the sweet love of Jesus that will come into your heart if you allow Him to enter with the Father and be Lord and Savior.

ഇൻൽ

He wants to bear you upon His chest just as the high priest bore the tribal stones on the BREASTPLATE of the ephod garment.

ഇൻൽ

He wants to bear you upon His chest just as the High priest bore the tribal stones on the BREASTPLATE of the ephod garment. He will carry you from the womb until your old age if you will allow Him. Let Him reveal who He is by giving Him the opportunity through simple trust, or faith in His Word.

One of the most precious promises in scripture spoken by Jesus is recounted by His disciple Matthew in the Gospels:

"Come unto me all ye that labor and are heavy laden and I will give you rest. Take my yoke upon you and learn of me; for I am meek and lowly in heart: and ye shall find rest for your souls. For my yoke is easy, and my burden is light." (Matt.11:28-30)

<u>The following prayer is only a model of one that can be prayed to receive Him for salvation:</u>

"Dear Jesus, I come to you just as I am without any pretense or special words. I ask you to come into my life and be my Savior and friend. I trust in your words that you came to the earth as a servant to die for me, and you rose from the dead.

I confess that I am a sinner in need of your help. You sacrificed yourself for me. I am sorry for my sins. I will no longer serve Satan, and I will turn from all disobedience that displeases you.

I believe you are the Christ and Son of the living God. Be Lord in my life, and lead me and guide me. I desire to know you better.

Thank you for living inside of me through Holy Spirit and receiving me as your child. I am saved and cleansed, and my sins are forgiven as of this day, and so I say, 'Thank you'. "

In Jesus' name…

8

PERSONAL REFLECTION & NOTES

8

PERSONAL REFLECTION & NOTES

9

SCRIPTURES & REFERENCES

Tribes of Israel	Scriptures
Judah — Jehovah to be praised (Jesus is our salvation)	*Isaiah 12: 2 / Luke 2:11, 25-32*
Reuben — behold a son (Jesus the son of God)	*Matthew 1:23 / Luke 2:7 / Hebrews 5:5*
Issachur — came as a servant (Jesus came to serve)	*Luke 2:49, 22:27*
Simeon — hearing/discernment (Jesus heard the voice of His Father and His instruction)	*Matthew 3:16-17/ John 8:40, 11:41-42/ Luke 2:40-52, 9:30-35*
Levi — joined (Jesus called 12 disciples to join Him in spreading the news of kingdom on the Earth)	*Luke 10:1-5, 9/ John 17:21-23/ 1 Corinthians 6:17*
Zebulun — dwelling (Jesus abiding in the Father and we in Him)	*John 14:10-11, 15:1-8, 10-14 / Matthew 12:17-21*

Tribes of Israel	Scriptures

Asher —
happy/blessed
(Jesus tells the Father that he fulfilled work
on Earth — kept men that God gave Him)

*John 15:10-14,
17:4-9, 12-13*

Naphtali —
wrestling in blessing
(Jesus received victory in Gethsemane)

*Luke 22:40-46 /
Hebrews 5:7-9*

Dan —
judgment ministered
(Jesus died for sins of mankind)

*Luke 24:46-48/
Romans 5:6-11*

Gad —
troop/breakthrough
(Jesus overcame death, hell/grave,
and enemy)

*Matthew 16:18 /
John 16:33 /
Revelation 1:18*

Joseph —
bountiful / increaser
(Jesus produced many sons)

*Romans 8:14 /
John 17:20-25*

Benjamin —
son of my right hand
(Jesus seated — right hand of the Father in
heaven making intercession)

*Luke 22:69/
Romans 8:34 /
Hebrews 7:25, 8:1*

Priestly Garment with Breastplate

www.gorepent.com
2010

King James Version Reference Bible
Zondervan

© 2004

Nelson's, New Illustrated Bible Dictionary
Robert F. Youngblood
Publisher, Thomas Nelson

© 1995

ABOUT THE AUTHOR

Pamela S. Cabell is a minister, seer, and teacher of the gospel — a born-again believer by the grace of God. She is also Holy Ghost filled and fire baptized. She received Christ away at college in 1979 at a small campus church called Monument of Hope. She loves the Lord dearly and has come to a deeper relationship with Him in recent years. It continues to be progressive; although as we all have experienced, there were some pitfalls along the way.

Pamela has three children, ranging in age from 28 to 32 years and are all saved and accepted Christ in their lives at young ages (answered prayer), as she was not brought up in the church. She is thankful for each of them. They will all do great things in the kingdom of God. She also has two-daughters-in-law, five grandchildren, and one more on the way.